BLOODWORK

by

Scott Zeidel

BLOODWORK
Copyright 2024 by Scott Zeidel

All rights reserved. No part of this book may be reproduced or transmitted in any form or by any means without written permission from the publisher, with the exception of brief quotations in a review.

Library of Congress Control Number: 2024949134
1. Poetry/General   2. Poetry/Animals and Nature
ISBN 13: 978-1-950750-54-2
ISBN 10: 1-950750-54-X

Cover art by Scott Zeidel

Title page graphic designed by jcomp on Freepik

Thomas-Jacob Publishing, LLC, Deltona, FL USA

Contact us at info@thomasjacobbooks.com

Dedicated to every animal and plant on the planet

Table of Contents

Bloodwork 1
Agates 3
Sugar 5
We'll Flower 7
Mockingbirds and Cats 9
The Building Inspector 11
Sleepers, Awake 13
Not Dancing 15
Devils and Fools 17
The Worst Was Possible 19
Two Poems For Smoky 21
The Stranger 23
Manistique 25
The Lover 27
Starry Night 29
The Funeral 31
Circular Reasoning 33
Two Doves 35
Water Haikus 37
A Scary Story 39
Lake and Moon 41
Good Luck 43

I'm An Opinion	45
Hot Biscuits	47
Sailing Through Time	49
A Remembrance	51
Tangled Arms	53
Forgotten Poppies and a Dead Sparrow	55
Seizure	57
The Narcissistic Artist Colony	59
My Favorite Things	61
Springlike	63
A Vein	65
Freedom!	67
About the Author	69
More Poetry from Scott Zeidel	71

Bloodwork

What happens
between a mother's
kiss and
loneliness?

I take my imagination for walks
through the waiting room
into photos
of forests, waterfalls, flowering
meadows,
surf.

I flop like a beached dolphin,
stuck by needles
so sharp they
can hardly be felt.

"Okay, sweetie,
keep this bandage on
for 30 minutes."

Agates

He dove into the northern lake,
ignoring the Siren's warning,
"The water's colder
than you think."

She sat on driftwood
admiring her collection of
Lake Superior agates,
polished flowers.

With blue lips
he dried on the sand,
and smacked a horsefly.

Brilliant sun,
waves drum,
she appeared at the car
without him.

Sugar

I'm on
a spinning needle
of soil and water,
stealing sweet kisses

from carrots and
peas in the garden—
sucrose shooting
through roots
like stars,

wild strawberries
by the river,
beets behind the shed,

afterwards
I lick the basket

We'll Flower

We're light

colors painted in
the passive voice

sand verbena pink,
emerald bays

sounds
echoing after death

we'll flower in sand dunes
watered by silence

Mockingbirds and Cats

I treasure animals
that remind me
of myself

—mockingbirds
speaking in tongues

house cats,
soft alien creatures,
who evolved to sleep
on the back of my couch

like Narcissus,
I gaze into a glassy puddle
looking for myself,
but seeing a mockingbird flying by

—on the ground
footprints from a
cat

The Building Inspector

A mockingbird
built a nest
in the brambles
of a cape honeysuckle
in my backyard.

He packed his beak
with detritus
from places unknown,
and fit them together
like Legos.

I sat, drank tea,
watching —
a building inspector,
half meditated, half protected him
from a Cooper's hawk.

He seemed to welcome my company.

Sometimes he perched close,
I could see his chest rising and falling —
at night I would hear him
through my window,
calling me.

Sleepers, Awake

Waiting for
consciousness

I slept through
conception,
birth,
at least one lifetime
and many dreams

I saw my embryonic
development happen
in reverse: first brain,
then toes, fingers, heart

I finally imploded into
the Big Bang

then rolled over
in my crib

Not Dancing

Martha & The Vandellas
danced in the street—
a shy boy who sat next to me
died in the jungle.

He had short hair,
breathy voice—
so soft you couldn't
hear him scream.

Devils and Fools

We're tarot cards,
devils and fools,
torn into random shards.

In lonely churchyards
we're nailed to wooden stools,
we're tarot cards.

Under exploding stars,
streaks of shooting molecules,
torn into random shards.

We're marred,
merely dried tears of ghouls,
we're tarot cards.

Misread and scarred,
to make the world seem cruel,
torn into random shards.

This reading we'll disregard,
forgetting to love fools.
We're tarot cards,
torn into random shards.

The Worst Was Possible

They flew above

a grounded
black-headed grosbeak
with broken wing

hidden under
an apple tree,
she survived on
rotten fruit

the worst was possible
as they circled
toward the ground

the grosbeak
spit out the apple seeds
—her wing would heal soon enough.

Two Poems For Smoky

I
She Breathes

She breathes
like a Mexican petunia,
a fiery chili, a ripe plantain
sizzling in coconut oil.

She breathes like a
Costa Rican iguana.

Challenge her if you like,
but beware:
there's no middleman,
she breathes like her garden.

II
A Bodhisattva

She's a bodhisattva,
her vibrations rest
on my windowsill,
they never decay,
just wait.

Sitting on the porch
in the evening,
lips puckered,
eyes half closed,
like the breeze.

Like a bird nest
filled with whistling babies
ready to fledge
from
above.

The Stranger

I saw a man
at a sidewalk cafe,
chips and salsa on his
blue tile table,
nervous sparrows danced
around his feet
to mariachi music.

He looked past me,
avoiding my stare.

A stranger.

His frog-like eyes,
swamp green, bulging,
were familiar. Seductive.

He bent over
and offered the birds
broken tortilla chips.

I leapt on a twin table
and landed, splash,
in a salted margarita.

When finished,
I hopped home behind him,
my home,
and introduced myself.

Manistique
(Summer, 1960)

I dug up a silver dollar
in the sands of Lake Michigan,
beneath a jungle gym.

In the summer
my family returned
to Douglas County, my birth place,
land of red clay, iron ore.

We stopped for Wonder
Bread sandwiches,
and to catch our breath
after crossing the Mackinac Bridge—
pylons above spruce trees
in clouds from which
workmen dropped.

Perch and pickerel
must have wondered why.

Gulls flew across the strait—
I dangled out the window
and gazed at the lake
through the open grid.

Our tires screamed
like workmen falling from the sky
like lost silver dollars.

The Lover

A critter
cowering beneath my bed,
with itty bitty eyes,
twinkling.

I built a labyrinth
from pillows
to my bedroom door.

Then clapped!

She shot by,
leaving pellets
and a broken heart.

Through my window
lit by the moon,
I could see her silky tail
in the grass,
like Cleopatra's asp.

Free at last.

Starry Night

I was too young
to be alone in the city—
Detroit, Michigan.

But there I was,
ghostlike,
standing before a LP.

The cover photo
was a hotrod
in a riot of stars.

I walked home
through dirty grass and snow,
dug up a cigar box
under a backyard maple
and withdrew my life savings.

Bought *Starry Night*
and earrings for a girl,
then wandered fields
below frosty constellations.

Oh, weeping stars,
swollen eyes!

In the summer
my family moved to California,
Detroit smoldered on the horizon
— the year was 1967.

Starry Night was
in the trunk of our car.

The Funeral

hollyhock blossoms
caught the breeze

and fell like rain
on the desert

verdins
sang a repetitive dirge,
a march

my parents' dust
fertilized the soil,
and dandelions bloomed yellow

Circular Reasoning

Nothing changed,
even after I drank
a cup of jimsonweed tea.

I ran through a palm oasis,
found myself
naked on my back
in a shallow pool—
a singing Phainopepla perched
on my belly. Tree frogs croaked—
the taste of nopales.

Or maybe not.

I wanted to starve myself ugly
till something changed—
I drank another cup,
chewed a lump of tea leaves
and saw the past before me.

I circled the oasis
singing Chuck Berry's
"Round and Round"
while the political were political.

Two Doves

they're not the same,
one's bigger,

sitting close

beaks open, preening,
nuzzling, feeding, kissing,
he's impatient

she's smaller
and builds the outline of a nest
in two dimensions, crossed
twigs

he coos

Water Haikus

I

In summer we swung
above the sleepy river
from willow branches.

II

Wounded red maple,
licking sap, sweetest nectar,
from her cherry lips.

III

Floating past my boat,
flowering water lilies
on the glassy lake.

IV

Empty idea
from the loudest croaking frog
in muddy puddle.

V

At this time of hate,
a log raft with idiots
shooting down rapids.

A Scary Story

Not all scary stories
are scary.

Camping
in the backyard,
the moon flew
through twinkling stars.

Under a sheet-draped picnic table
with Boy Scout knife, chocolate bar,
flashlight.

Tomatoes were red,
soft, plentiful —
when fired across
the fence with hate,
faux blood dripped.

Lightning and
thunder shook the greenery,
— we joined hands, circled,
and howled like coyotes.

Lake and Moon

From the pump by the lake,
I filled a tin cup
with iron water
filtered through the earth.

Then swallow
with one gulp.

I caught the moon
in an empty cup
and waded along the shore,
minnows tickled my legs,
sand between my toes.

Galaxies sailed across
the glassy water.

I dropped the moon in the lake,
and it floated away,
glowing like a Chinese lantern.

Good Luck

reforested,
replanted,
regrown

memories dissolve
as the wind
reads us
a bedtime story

what's important after all,
even bodies burn?

we burst into light
with a pat on the butt

I'm An Opinion

don't hurt me
—I'm confused

climbing out of existence,
one step at a time,
with memories, fragments,
thoughts in tow

I'm an opinion,
a mood

don't hold that against me,
'cause my dreams are calloused

I'm just a screaming bunny
hanging in the sky
from the talons of a hawk

don't hurt me

especially now after
the hawk dropped me
in an oasis
where fungi live
in the shadows

Hot Biscuits

Stare at a blank page
till you see a wooded idyll
deep in dogwoods —

Close your eyes
and hold the moment.

Eat hot biscuits
slathered in butter
and sourwood
mountain honey.

Time to cross
the finish line
as cherubs pluck lutes
in sweet euphony.

Sailing Through Time

Today Violet is born.

Billions of galaxies
and a single grain of sand
hidden in the crease of
her smile.

Volcanic jungles
with all earth's flowers,
sailing through time
on Noah's spaceship
protected by light years of grace
on a breeze of joy.

Delivered one day
under an evergreen
in the garden.

Today Violet is born.

A Remembrance

Something was wrong—

She had stopped
sleeping with Squirrelly,
her stuffed animal.

Normally they
snuggled together
on cold nights.

Siamese,
with icicle eyes
that sparkled across steep
wintery dunes.

Left beneath
a cloak of cumuli,
trying to remember.

The lone survivor
rose out of the cloud
to take her place
on the back of my couch,
frozen and bewildered,
as if she'd just
seen a ghost.

Tangled Arms

Tangled arms and legs and
lips and tongues.

I tried to make a difference,
behind a desk, arms waving,

after my knees hit the ground,
crying like a baby,

worried and sleepy
(it was difficult becoming a man),

I allowed myself to close my eyes,
and made a decision:

I picked myself up
and shuffled home.

Forgotten Poppies and a Dead Sparrow

in search of spring poppies,
I passed the Whiskey on Sunset Boulevard,
turned right at the coast
Santa Ana breeze over the ocean,
Hendrix on the radio,
orange carpet of sunburned kelp
like a bed of poppies

returned home
to find a dead sparrow
on the driveway

dug a hole
with bare hands
in my marigold garden

buried her,
while growling
like a German shepherd

Seizure

I gave a lecture many moons ago,
the words swirled off the board above my class
and rose into stars of a sparkling glow,
the sky above a field of blowing grass.
A psychedelic spasm, though unsure,
the colorful natural scene one dreams of,
or floating shapes that melt into a blur,
like rain drops from a puffy cloud above.
I fell into a deep and empty well,
my tears and cries remain in the pitch dark,
they barely vibrate in this empty shell,
like quiet singing of a meadow lark.
After learning to chew this bitter pill,
avoid discomfort, sacrifice freewill.

The Narcissistic Artist Colony

severe, unsmiling,
hair shines like
dime store fire trucks

diet of strange fruit,
prickly pear glochids,
genetically modified mushrooms

too creative
self-portraits
line the walls

they even sleep together

My Favorite Things

I don't care about things,
opinions, thoughts, beliefs.

I don't care about
tastes, styles, suitability, values,
uniqueness, rarity, strength.

Must you think, weigh, measure,
analyze, evaluate, chart, graph, grade,
compete, complete?

'cause there's a path out back
where toes will find
blackberries lining
an oak shaded creek.

Springlike

Oregano blossoms—
and honeybees,
marine blue butterflies,

sip the flavor
of a watered garden.

and the memory—
joyful tears
and celebration,

dripping flowers
above warm soil.

fluttering through cloudy pollen,
everything tastes springlike,

even dandelions.

A Vein

There's a vein
that runs through my arm—

It was there at birth,
and it's still there,
hidden within a wrinkle.

It carries ideas,
lies, truths,
intolerances,
diffused points of view.

And giraffes,
water buffalos,
a bloody lamb,
etched granite,
petroglyphs.

There's a vein
that runs through my arm
like a stream,
like my life.

Freedom!

Richie Havens
sang at Woodstock.

"Freedom, freedom!"

Crows cawed from above,
"Freedom, freedom!"

A lonely
motherless child,
hung his thumb
from the neck of the guitar,
—like a rope.

And a boy,
just graduated from high school,
watched from the grass,
knowing full well
that his time had come,
grabbed a crow's tail,
and took off before it was too late.

About the Author

Scott was born in Northern Wisconsin in 1951 and grew up in Detroit, Michigan and the Southern California desert. He is a child of the 60s and still believes in a world of peace, love, and understanding. He spent many years in academia, both as a student and a teacher. Now retired, he spends his time walking in his beloved desert, writing poetry, painting, and playing the guitar. He is married to Smoky, an avid gardener and writer, and has all kinds of wonderful children and grandchildren. *Bloodwork* is his second poetry collection. His first, *Welcome*, was also published by Thomas-Jacob Publishing.

Scott's poetry is quite diverse in style, from very short haikus and other brief memories, to longer open forms. His favorite poets are William Carlos Williams and Allen Ginsberg. Almost all his poetry, from shorter works like "Bloodwork" and "Not Dancing" to longer compositions like "Starry Night," is based on true stories. Some of his poetry is in an older traditional design—"Seizure," for example, is a sonnet and "Devils and Fools" is a villanelle.

More Poetry from Scott Zeidel

Welcome, by Scott Zeidel, is also available from all major online bookstores in both print and ebook formats.

www.ingramcontent.com/pod-product-compliance
Lightning Source LLC
LaVergne TN
LVHW052339080426
835508LV00044B/2652